Razzy Dazzy Spasm Band

Razzy Dazzy Spasm Band

There is here an expressed challenge to form and content while embracing form and content and still to write in a poetic genre. As such, it is jazz. Razzy Dazzy Jazzy—

Michael Klumpp

ISBN: 9798691784781

This book is Volume 2 of the *Klumpp Chaps*, a chapbook series published by Wick House Publishing.

Wick House Publishing
1443 Bubbling Brook Ct.
Fort Collins, CO 80521

God told me to write this poem and I could go to bed – so i will:

You do not understand madness
Unless you are mad
It is
A synthesis
Quite unlike it

See

I cannot tell if the hall is
Five feet long or short
Or if short is long or short
Or if
The glass door into the kitchen
Is
Really
Or is not
Or
It is a door into a dream I never saw but was in

Where some ex
People of
Some ex life
Crawled on hands and knees
And
Where both in the next
And in some other word

Madness

The black and white tile
Was pink and white
Or
Was it my shoes
Vans

This is so sad
I cannot tell
If I am real or not
Or if
You are
Or not
Or
Anything

Imagine music
(I know I do)
somehow
it is an embrace

or
the soft edge
of a silk
scarf
or perceptible reality
drag
drugged
across the calf
of my leg
just the calf
at night
in the dark
or actually the grey moon light

was it an apple
or just some fruit

eve
preferred not to eat alone

we have begun something here
we cannot stop

my cat is croaking
with a horse cracked meow

this devastating reality
this slip in time

tomorrow I get coffee
it is something I really enjoy.

"darling be home soon"

you and i
we can't be at peace

not
because of you

it is the extinguishing
    remarks
  of all
      said
        things

leaves fall in fall
grow in spring
        i like soup.

c

in windows of my soul
i see her
she sees me
we see each to the other

sad day
falling upon my head
and no memory
no Knowledge
no one
nothing

no more.

for mike doughty and hong kong in winter rain:

the twill and twiddle
twirling thumbs drum about the middle
essentially circling and circling
no rhyme or reason
motion and motion and motion forgotten
hands in laps like eyes to the ethereal
like sitting lotus
like
sitting mystic
sitting mysteriously
folding legs triangular
dynamic like a pyramid standing still

i think hot sand
feels good on rich brown skin
tanning in the coconut smell
white and creamy until rubbed in a dreammy
surfing the curling thumbs of the sick sea
green and blue
rolling white and white and washed away

the fingernails
of a mans hands who
was on the street
he
had nails
so clean in photo negative
grease oil stained
not like van gogh
oil or dali dough
or
weakness
but
oil like broke and poor and working too hard to
turn thumbs upon mirrors
but he is
he just doesn't know it

we all want coffee at the diner and a cigarette after dinner
sex upon a sunday morning and flowers after fall leaves
rain before our sunshine and mossy grey green mornings in irish spring
wisteria and hysteria
we don't want cuts on anything
no less but more and yet

twill and twiddle
thumbs turning 'round the middle
little flesh fans burning energy

and an effigy
of nothing.
love may be beautiful but all sound dissipates in half lives lingering long
after it's gone.

crush on a pole dancer:

hardcore -
rage simmering
waist on the pants too high
corn on the toe
one shoe too tight
or one too loose
can't get it even, Steven - gotta lump on one sock,
heal outa place
no face
deadpan voice - what does it matter
the hatter mad
dealing from the bottom of the deck
pulling cards from his hat
cat grinning
exit into the sun
kick the blue fender
smell the dew on cinderblock behind the club
i need sleep
not another cigarette.

the journey:

the journey
toil and trouble
bubble
up
pop!
stop
who taught you to be on top -
love is love
and hate is hate
- on the top or on the bottom
fade-
traveling-
what street is this
is this hong kong new orleans chicago dallas atlanta san fransisco nairobi
or stralsund
from the alley - even dighton looks the same -
i had a tree outside my window
winter cold wind
creeping in on paper angel wings
like the fibered touch of dragon flies
crispy and crinkles
stars that twinkle
night in a desert
like night in a field
or the moon sealed the deal
grass whispers
leaves cackled
dry leaves crackled
oak burning in the gutter on saturday morning
before we melted the ice cap-
i am my father's dinosaur
he is old and i am little he is gone
and i am old and you are little and you are big and i am going
sailing across the smooth grey lake of pontchartrain
insane to ride the wind like that
cast to the side - screaming like fire as we glide along
song singing in my head on the long walk home-
earlier tonight we ran from the law
because we wanted to
and upon too much to drink - did
to the fuck and folly of it all
with our balls slung upon our chests
no man's dance -
our strut of freedom young and proud - loud
and making love is making love
on the top or bottom -
hate is hate - smokem if you gottem
see
you can lie still or you can moan

sleep next to someone or play alone
but this is your one roll
one curve of the wave - rave
one change to dance with mushrooms and hookahs
this is your one day to visit this parade
ichi go and ichi e
this is your t-shirt
your oxford
your robe your cloth dress
wear it until the sweat stains spread their wings
and declare
we are worn
we have been worn
are torn are tattered
did it all as though it mattered
 and retreat upon the wind -
'cause making love is making love
on the top or on the bottom -
there is something to savor
- to remember
this december
and close the window
- wwwwwwwwwiiiiiiiiiiiiinnnnnnnddddddddd.
!

ribbon:

a ribbon
blowing in the wind
blue like the sky
light and carefree
blown from the hair
of a woman
hanging
by a rope
kicked the chair
and said
goodbye

paregoric was my mother:

i never learned to share

it was the paregoric
mine
my blanket
sweet childhood of no mother's breast
instead
tincture of opium
anhydrous morphine
god of the little gee
my friend
my friend my friend

my mother my friend my opiate
allahloowya
bloof

bublea
bublea
boof

i am so much the need for all i want
put me back to bed
i will not cry my loneliness away
with the tincture
my anhydrous muscle
my

life
began this way

you cannot share
what you never had
what
was never
real
anyway

like love
or mornings

or breast milk.

why rain and wet grass make me sad (it is because of string that i went mad):

if ever
i was young and wet
because of rain
and standing in the grass
feeling the tongues lick on my lost legs
the earth saturated
could consume no more
i was little
tiny
a child lost on the surface of God's damp earth
raining
i remember
raining
if ever i was lost
and wet
i was young

then and never again
alive or dead
broken
like some string

clouds hang in grey
fog
in greyfog
in grey light of haze and fog
and rain
and wet
the endless wet earth that seems alive and about to burst

i am damned
i am undamned
i am damp

what of it Jesus?
what of my childhood and such memories of grey and wet and earth and
time
what of it

i remember the smell distinctly
wet sheetrock
wet wood
wet concrete

we are not outside! we are in this humid growth of life
and there is some structure
filled with dust and webs
it is old here

and dirty

i wish i could tell you i did not know what it was like under bridges
at the back in the damp where the dirt meets the concrete and steel
where there is no sky
where there is no one who is well
we don't go there to be well
but to be hidden
hidden from our own lives
heroin
and eyes closed
it is death alive lonely there where no one goes
i wish i could tell you i didn't know

i wish i could tell you so much
but my fall has been great and great is the sense of falling and long and i
remember each throttled second
each joyous contribution of terror as
i was declining life at 32 ft per sec per sec
flying by
dropping from heaven
a lightnight bolt

what can i say
i never had sex with the dead?
how does that free me?
i did not eat the dead?
oh my, i am blessed - i did not eat or have sex with the dead

all other crimes are mine -
i walk with all beasts
i die with all daemons
i dine with all sinners
i lie down in the dust and am dust

dust
dust?
dust is not damp
dust is not wet
dust is dry!

i am saved.

but only until i remember again
what it feels like to be damp
and again i am sailing down
falling
and damned
near the base of the tree
on this damp earth
i will lie down and die.

eat me.
feel my breasts.
now we are all dead together.

if ever i was young
and wet
and standing in the wet green grass.

broken beyond words but not beyond the pain of communication:

sssssssssssss

lllll

lllll

ssssssssssssssss

fu fff fu

lllllll

sssssssssss

Across a sea of time and confusion:

Across a sea of time and confusion
Signals become mixed

"and as he turned to his down wind leg to land…"

the little girl
stirred silent against a surreal landscape
of dirt and death

behind her
the clean walls of a courtyard
stone upon stone
mud heat and time
transformed
inside
the angel of death sat in black with her mother
negotiating a time of departure

"you could tell something was wrong…"

the wings draped still at the side of the messenger
concern in her eyes
"I will help you – I will remove all pain.
Tell me what you want"

"care for my children, they have nothing"

"the wings shook suddenly and there was smoke…"

"cover me with your vail, sweet angel – black upon black and silence"

"then it hit the ground."

In the kibera slums – HIV, the tears of children and the hands of God.

a bad drug induced dream:

there is a dry heat
which comes from a space heater
gas
and an orange light
sets
like a heavy hue
over the darkness

and i can see her eyes
nothing else
but her eye
and they move and change
inside a kaleidoscope
twisting
eyes

i had a dream
filled with demons
eating a corpse
supping on its crooked grey penis

they looked up as i woke
wondering how i crossed from world to world
asleep and awake at the same time
dreaming in both worlds
attacked and attached
to each nightmarish
face

the demons looking at me
and of course
i looked back
wishing to also be eating the dead
necrophilia

it was the opium

my poor nephew is dying
drug addicted
toothless
and gone.

forget the ducks:

time
sequence
click
flap

ducks and monkeys
winged monkeys
winged monkeys with screwdrivers

working on engines and door hinges
coconut breath and kahlua
little paper parasols

who the hell said "monkeys"

tell them to put down the tools
        and back away
                from the
                    engine.

"monkeys, you're not welcome here if
        you won't behave."

canine teeth and chimp chatter screams
red eyed monkeys

old monkeys
sitting around an outdoor table
in lawn chairs
    on the deck
laughing monkey laughs
and telling stories
drinking salty dogs and bloody marys
mrs monkeys
in short skirts and bikini tops
with big straw hats and sunglasses
serving brunch
        fruit salad and banana smoothies

oh
to be a monkey
    when the work it done.

when we fed the cat:

when we fed the cat
we had no idea
he'ld be back

we had no notion
of the ocean
and it's high flight patterns for birds
in search of lost lands

what we didn't know
was what we didn't know
was what we didn't know we didn't know

we didn't know

still

the cause and effect ran its course
the fans stood around in remorse
the rider came upon a white horse
and all anyone saw was nothing

flow:

flow
like water
soft cold tongues
chattering against rock
rolling and twisting free

winter's stream
falling from the snowy heights
beneath stone
countering each dead end
in crystal and tenderness

down and out
from a perch upon the sky
to a blood warm bed in the sea.

this is the path etched by too much love.

St Stanislaus:

height
from which i can fall
is nothing
to the depths
from which i can rise

platitudinous virgins
original to the core
segment
ritual
and despised for genius

each
prophet of
each
thought of each

breathing
and walking erect
does not
make you human

love once
at all times
everything

elves make gifts
at christmas

i am saint stanislaus and my fever is rising.

Attention Deficit Order:

There is static
In my forehead

It drifts and sifts
Down
Into the person below myself
(the body beneath my head)

-i am beneath myself-

which then of course reflects
that

I am above myself –

But
This
However
Is not about that

There is a static
In my forehead
Which clutters
The pathways to nirvana
Forging out from the sides of my
Numbskull
(I miss the stooges)
like spikes driving out
from within my head
nails on the blackboard of me the head of which I am
and is the head of which is me

but
this
nonetheless
is not about that

but
about
the static which
drifts from beneath my forehead
to cover the crown of my head
like cooking oil
on a hot skillet
standing and moving
dancing in the heat
and smoking

dyslexia and ADD

adhd

how many words can you make with the combination

sex
ad
had
exel
syli
sad

this is the clutter
the static
the madness
which prevents me from even telling you
about something I forgot long ago
when I decided to write

what you doin'?

Bipolar:

hate blisters
the skin like fire
the soul like ice
the self like refreshing

masochism
the love of self hatred
the self of love hatred
the hatred of self love
hatred in the love of self
the love of self in hatred
confusion

one preposition away from truth

God spoke
separating light from dark
interrupting confusion and chaos
God is not bipolar

i hate myself
it is the only pure form of love i know.

thump:

thump, thump, thump

dogs tail on a wooden floor
heart within the chest of a loved one
knock on the door

quiet

the sound of no one answering

drinking sake:

i am small
(not light)
small

i am small

i smell
(not smell)
but detect odors

i smell

and i can think
of things

i can even think i think profound things
(but who knows – who will be the judge)
don't we all

i can be riveted with joy
in an instant
or fall from the clouds
to burn in the earth's core
in an instant

moody? or miraculous?
or doesn't matter at all?

where will you be - ?
at that instant?
surrounded by family singing hymns
alone on the bathroom flood gasping
crushed steel and velvet
sacrificed at the alter of ideology
marching into mayhem
throwing yourself upon a grenade
(thank you mike monsoor)
or sleeping deeply – uhoh – seeya'
?

does an educated guess
equal
deification
under the primordial system of the smartest man wins
or was it might makes right or
was the might the might of the mind
or the strength of the will or the ability to crack nuts
with bear hands

i love bar-b-que
sacks of weasels
help the wise man help himself
tweezers
i feel sick –

look!
behind you!
the moment is now –

did you pray
or reach for your glass?

what does it matter?

we didn't mean to:

we didn't mean to
spend our whole lives
inside
working
when outside
pulsing
was the heartbeat
of the universe
glowing

it was the first visible talisman
pointing the way to God

now we are old

please
let me be like ash
in the wind.

Mother:

mother comes
and her soft scented hands
brush away the tears
age
and the fears of growing old

mother comes
and i can breath again for a moment
seeing her hands
and the tenderness of her touch

mother comes
and the darkness runs
like mascara on crying eyes
through powdered cheeks
down to the soft skin beneath my chin.

the diminished:

the diminished
wind of a voice
quiet unto silence undo darkness unto peace
begat night begat another fucking day

do you like the way they color empty space in 0's and 1's and create life
images more real than real
that byte with real teeth (oh yes i did)
toggle on
toggle off
creating depth
volume
time and space
other worlds
other places

i used to drink
now i prefer opiates in small doses

morning in paradise:

there is almost no passion left
for flesh or paper
(whatever)
folded hands
folded legs
and a navel which sucks light from baby chickens
and shits black stones into tan tien

i am bile and cinders
died little by little
dying even more

it is a journey of numbness
sinking into a dispassionate void
i cared once
twice
bounced of the bottom and traveled to the surface
three!

i will not see the surface again
unless rescued by some other arms
i have forgotten to swim
no will to hold my breath
taking water into weary lungs
the burn and blackout are bliss.

1-24-10

someone coming:

there's someone coming who can't be see
carrying a can of gasoline
they'll torch this place like a bright red dream
there's someone coming who can't be seen

there's someone coming whose not real well
riding on the wings of hell
i hope they'll sit and rest a spell
there's someone coming whose not real well

not that you would notice:

i recognize the symptoms
of my depression
turning inside like so many maggots
in a composting toilet

i remember sitting in the dark
in my car
on the roadside
wanting only
to disappear
or pick up the scent of some passing motorist
finding substance
in the whatever of what they were chasing
maybe they know where we are going

i didn't know
until the doctor told me
that i was depressed
it never occurred to me that i had not laughed
in three years

broken men
do not advance the clock
the well make it tick
our culture has no need for the leftover pieces
use what works
dismiss the rest

how are you feeling today?
not as you would notice.

Poem For Alan Addotto
the twisted steel strings of a guitar:

bent
twisted
tied
and tightened

sound

vibrations

i remember sitting backstage
poor david's pub – dallas
she was touring
city to city
trying to make a name
living out of her car
guitar
rising star
her hair long
flowing
like a mane

she hid beneath the bangs

on the stage
a cowboy poet
ranting chanting
rhyming to a dark room

 it was cold that night
a friend's dog was recently dead
another friend
trying to move forward
i was there to read poetry to improved music
theologian wounded and wandering
Shi-de searching for Hanshan

 everything was wrong where once it had all been right

my life has had so many days
i have been here for most of them
but i was not there then
and have been searching ever since.

Hanshan – i have come to the coast of China crying for you
i die and rise again and die and rise again
each moment of each day of each tear in time

Hanshan – the moon
is the string of my lute
the mane of the horse
tightened

and i am lonely without you.

dancing

like an old man with one limp leg
my friend

that night
i left the pub
sat in my car and cried

the sad sad girl
on her journey from alaska
in pursuit of fame – she made it

the cowboy poet just wanted to be heard
the dog is still dead (in this world)
his owner lost forever
improve?
it's all i know to do.

i am drinking cardamom tea
in hong kong

the clouds hang upon the mountains

tightened
tied
and
twisted

.

Revisionists:

in the caves
at night
we would take coals
from the edge of the fire
and draw

my favorite was a four legged chicken
another a crocodile head with an elephant body

everyone would laugh

next night
often in another cave
i'ld draw ritual sacrifice of a virgin
a virgin, mind you -
who in their right mind would waste a good virgin?
she might be surrounded by a host of pregnant women
like they were jealous of her firm breasts
well, there's often some truth even in jest – ha!

cave drawings – they were the best.

i wonder,
what ever became of those -

slipping:

i walk into a doorway
traveling from one room to another
but
when i leave the living room
to go into the bathroom
i step through the doorway
and arrive on the porch
i am eighty
screaming at the cat
to get away from the bird feeder
i turn to go into the kitchen
and am standing before the wall
in my daughter's room
face to face
with the dark reality
that
this is madness

i see between thoughts
the thoughts i would have if
i were at a pace slightly ahead
or slightly behind
myself

where the reality of everything changes

it didn't happen this way or that
because
it wasn't this way or that
and in the end of it all
when i sleep
i wait to wake in the past

but of course
i never do

lately
when i watch a movie at night at home
the reflection on the glass against the night
confuses me
am i in this world or that
to the left looking in
or on the right looking out.

time

it's just a shot away

visit the crypt
walk through the end of time
with a candle
shrinking from shadows and the cold cold draft
moving by life a fish in black water
flickering little devil
time and light
the candle
wax drips onto the hand
white and warm
like some milky stiff cum
oozing down the long length of a dead white penis
necrophilia

its always been this way
sometimes you see them sometimes you don't
the shadows move with the light
there is the reflection of something outside inside on the glass
the curtain sways and the room elongates
fear stands in boots
square in the chest
hard to breath
pulse totally unnecessary

much the same as ts elliot walking down the stairs
whistling aimlessly while musing over the lines of ash wednesday
it's all so cute
life and death and all
time and deep space
the curve in the window at the back of the room
and the horror of loneliness

loneliness unlike the stuff of life
alone so complete
that there is a vacuum of human conscience
you can fuck your dead neighbor
and drink chocolate milk from a dogs skull

we called him poppy
he had a little round head
she could quite pronounce puppy
white dripped from his eyes
we collected it
dried it
and tried it
it was no poppy
so we ate him

it is always we
when we get so broken
i becomes so many
it cures the loneliness when we are
because then there is a witness to tell me later
we all could have done it
we all understand
we all love you
we needed that
we need you to sleep now
sleep

that's the way the sickness comes

it's just a shot away

time.

Stealth:

in the hall
by the phone
there's a pad
with a number

on the porch
there's a stand
for a flag

in the sky
there's a place
for a cloud
and a smile

my shoes are old and tight
i rest them in luke warm water at night
but i have slippers for the morning cold
and to keep the small things from sticking to my feet

the odor of coffee and figs
is as old as her duster

what was it you wanted?

the drip:

the drip
drips
on my foot
(something about that drip)
the tub is now empty
(something about that drip)
the tree
all i want to do is trim the tree
the drip
sitting in the tub
(what is it)
the drip
my foot
the tree
when i trimmed the tree
i was invisible
i was Shi Ti
bonsi dancing
the drip
(what is it about the drip)

the water is hot!

silly ding:

ding – the bell – speaks

zzzzzzzzzziiiiiiiinnnnnnnngggggggggggggggggggggggggggggggggg

delta wave
heart chakra singing

zzzzzzzzzzziiiiiiiiiiiiiiiiiiiiiiiiiinnnnnnnnnnnnnnnnnnnngggggggggggggg
gg

he says – welcome – to a broken world
nothing to fear
it is just that way

zzzzzzzzzzzzzzzziiiiiiiiiiiiiiiiiiiiiiiiiiiiiiiiiiiiiinnnnnnnnnnnnnnnnggggggggg
ggg

he says – it makes the heart heavy unless you are well rooted
then, you understand
that heaven and earth
are just as they are
it is expectation that is wounded

zzzzzzzzzzziiiiiiiiiiiiiiinnnnnnnnnnnnnnnnnnnnnnnngggggggggggg

let your expectation go – he says
all is love

silly ding -

.

folly:

this is insane
i have seem
my mother and my father
walking
in fields of fire
burning and not burning

life
fragile
frail

life
flowing
like water
flowing
time
flowing
all one river timelifewaterwonder and what of God?

life
this is insane
i am afraid that i have wasted every measure of every day

hesitation
i have hesitated to love God
in total spirit and devotion
i have neglected the light on the water
i have hesitated
and time and life
have flown

folly
life is folly
to die is folly
to breath is folly
to embrace morning and the beauty of a thousand sunsets
is folly

folly is folly
no folly is folly
unfolly is folly
follyness is folly
folly followed by folly is folly is folly is folly

folly

oh my God
forgive me

i am dying and do not want to die
i am living and do not want to die
i am breathing and do not want to die
i am dying
forgive me
and let me eat some ice cream
i love the taste of ice cream
i sometimes eat it with nuts and caramel
sometimes i eat too much
the sugar gives me migraines
then my eyes hurt on the inside
i get dizzy and want to throw up then cry
God, how i love ice cream
(i could do without it but i really like it
it's just ice cream, after all)

would it be folly to have an orange soda instead?

Wrapping:

Wrapping rice in sea weed
Wrapping tears in rich blue sky
Wasted days upon an empty stage
Dust and a clutch with a fake gold chain
Sequin and empty
Not even a ribbon for someones long forgotten hair

I miss my father more and more
Maybe that is what will draw me in
The fade of light
The dissolve to gray
Light up on fred and michael
All too dead and laughter

It comes for those who miss the past more than the future
My sons and daughters
Must walk and walk and walk some more
Green and gold upon the trusnks of trees
Lit with camera angle sweet light and timeless
Ah – they have their sons and daughters and sons and daughters

Oyster shells
On sea walls
Revealed
As the tide goes out
And my arms lay empty
Upon my cold cold chest.

The wind.

one thousand:

i remember
(don't think that i don't)
when it rained and we listened to the radio
in a parked car
and

records (we did) in your bedroom
sitting on the shag carpet
gold
at the foot of your bed
hi fi
and God
the Father and all
took to making
the heavens and the earth and stuff and
   i
remember when
(don't think that i don't)
you sat
   at
the piano
playing
(because i do – i can still touch items in the room – like the embroidered
throw pillow with gold piping)
i am no madman
    but

move through time and
    space

some

sifting mostly
   - but i digress – the point is not my movement or pillows or even
remembering

what then?

hmmm

see

i remember
things
clips
leaves as they crackle walking trails in tennessee
the smell of pine needles
or

bamboo burning at the back yard of my
        parents' home

i remember you
in silence
one thousand pictures of you
one thousand smells
and touches
one thousand nights
without you
i remember my death
and it hasn't happened

how is that?

light

He said light
and pow!
but lately
all i remember is darkness-

pancreas
- now there's a funny
word,

almost home:

cast your hope on Miughalaigh
the journey draws to a close
we can steer home from here

kittiwakes, puffins and razorbills
circle out to sea and back
come home to your nests and night my friends
cast you hope on Miughalaigh

we've beat the beast of the sea
one more time
and we're headed in for bed and bowl

then out to sea again we roll

no one stands upon the waves
but wastes away
in salt and sea
the horizon calling
to the ghost of God

cast your hope on Miughalaigh
we're almost home
and almost gone.

www.ingramcontent.com/pod-product-compliance
Lightning Source LLC
Chambersburg PA
CBHW020515160726
47991CB00007B/2960